FROM DIRT PATHS

to

GOLDEN STREETS

Poems of Immigrant Experiences

Merle Fischlowitz

authorHOUSE®

AuthorHouse™
1663 Liberty Drive
Bloomington, IN 47403
www.authorhouse.com
Phone: 1-800-839-8640

First published by AuthorHouse 11/15/2010

ISBN: 978-1-4520-8455-8 (sc)
ISBN: 978-1-4520-8457-2 (e)

Printed in the United States of America

This book is printed on acid-free paper.

Certain stock imagery © Thinkstock.

ACKNOWLEDGEMENTS

Many of these poems passed through the caring hands of fellow poets before the first edition in 1999. Among others, I particularly thank a teacher and mentor, Hayley Mitchell, who published "Soup" in Sheila-Na-Gig, Vol. 13, spring 1999.

The poem "Soup" has also been published in *Good Company: Poets from Grinnell College,* J. Kissane, editor, Grinnell College Press, 2000 and *New Harvest: Jewish Writing in St. Louis,* H. Schwartz, editor, Brodsky Library Press, 2005.

In preparation for this second edition, my friend and poet Megan Webster has helped with excellent editorial critique, and I have received additional editorial assistance from Melanie Dellas.

My wife, Teresa, was the source of several stories. She has given me unending support and inspiration for my work.

Cover illustration by Benjamin P. Fischlowitz

FOREWORD

These poems, written from 1962 to 2009, are mostly individual stories of immigration to our land. The title tells my bias: that people all around the world see the United States, if not a land of golden streets, at least as a land of golden opportunities.

Poems in the first part of the book focus on European immigration. Some poems are fiction, barely removed from reality, while others are taken from family tales and stories of other immigrant friends. Holocaust survivors' stories were sources for several poems: "Hedda," "A Wedding Gift," "Bonds," "Soup," and "Am Yisrael Chai!"

Poems in the latter part of the book tell stories of individual immigrants from other cultures whom I have personally known or read about: Arabic, "Customs;" East African, "Somalia in San Diego;" Japanese, "At Manzanar;" Korean, "What's Cooked Up For Me?" Mexican, "On the Mountain," "Golden Wheat" and "Port of Entry;" Russian, "Maxima;" and Vietnamese, "Reach Tomorrow." Many of these poems are told in the voices of immigrants from those varied lands.

Poems new in this second edition are "Golden Wheat," "Maxima," and "Somalia in San Diego."

CONTENTS

BLOOD AND GOLD

The path was muddy from spring rain,
and the blood hardly showed as it ran
down the gully from the shul past his house.
He knew each year someone would be struck.
Either at Passover or Easter local folk
would have recreational revenge
for the thought that his ancestors, so long ago,
had killed their Son of God.
Now it was his son who lay in pain at home
on a straw bed. Eli, Eli,
he thought, how many more years
must I wait and hope for deliverance,
for peace to come to this small town?

No more waiting! He resolved instead
to wrap up his few things, his family,
his life and memories, and go
to the new land, the "Goldeneh Medina,"
where his wife could light candlesticks
in peace, where his children need not fear
a stranger on the street. After Pesach
they wrapped all their precious things,
gave away the extra food to those in need,
swept clean the house, now empty
of hopes and dreams and tears.
Walking first, then a wagon to the train;
a train to the port, then a stinking, rocking ship.
A working peddler in New York crowds;
from a fourth-floor, three-room home,
he sought to pave his own golden streets.

"Eli, Eli," Hebrew, "My God, my God."
"Goldeneh Medina," Yiddish, "Golden Land."

CANDLESTICKS

The letter took four weeks crossing the Atlantic
to tell my grandfather
of his mother's weakened pulse.
He was gone three months from new land,
new home and family, to care for,
to bury and to mourn. On his return
he brought his wife silver candlesticks
for Sabbath lights.

Today I can call across the miles to learn
of my mother's pulse, her smile and appetite,
and so decide if I should make a four-hour flight
to visit her in the nursing home.

I can also call my granddaughters
to learn about their school, their play,
their Hebrew lessons and their dance.

Dare I think the pulse of life allows
that in years to come, I will be able
to give Sabbath candlesticks
for a granddaughter's table?

TO MY GRANDSON

I dared the ocean that you
might be born to my son,
so you could roam the golden streets I walked
to save bus fare going to my first job.

I left a beautiful ancient city,
fleeing before a Czar's army found me,
or cries of Hep! Hep! echoed
in blows upon my head,
that you might choose to wear
or not to wear tradition's cap
when, or if, you pray.

I carried my parents' picture –
gray-bearded, black-capped father,
full and proudly fed mother –
as my private souvenir.

I proudly sat with you at play,
lighting Shabbat candles, or any day,
for any ready camera
to give you memories.

Now a tired man of sixty-three,
I see the brightness of your eyes,
the zest of seven years of life,
and I give in
and rest.

"Hep," an acronym for the Latin meaning "Jerusalem is lost;" a cry used by Russian thugs in anti-Semitic pogroms.

GRADUATION

In a book-lined room of a university
rising from the American prairie
I saw him read a Polish-language newspaper.

Surging sinews of face and arm,
concrete wrinkles round his steely eyes,
hard-calloused hands,
set him apart from the softened seers
of the book-lined room.

His labor's dirt scrubbed away,
the inexpensive suit, proudly bought
for this graduation day,
sits well on his muscled frame.

With careful glance he seeks to know anew
his full-bloomed daughter, who, in joy,
has loosed her academic robe.

Black robe with tasseled cap
and this festive day
replaced the discount-store dresses,
the frugal meals, the misered baths
he took to wash away steel mill's grime.

And then his eyes returned to read
his Polish-language newspaper
in a book-lined room
of an American prairie university.

I wondered how my grandfather felt
at my father's college graduation.

INHERITANCE

Out from under his grandfather's peddler pack,
with skilled hands of his cabinetmaker father;

nourished by four centuries
of learned men;
schooled to overcome
his immigrant inheritance,
trained to conquer an alien world;

he left behind
      the peddler's pack,
      the cabinet shop,
and learned elders' rituals.

In the conquered, alien world,
now his own,
his children inherit
five centuries of learned men
and unbroken traditions
from the cabinetmaker's son.

For my father's last birthday, January 1969.

WRINKLED

Mother washed and wrinkled our clothes
so they would not look new as we left our town,
after she had sold the house and farm.
All the money she had saved she spent
on clothes, shoes, silverware and such –
so the customs police wouldn't find any cash
to steal from us.

BAGELS

Brisket and matza balls,
roast chicken and noodle pudding
are too heavy, too old-fashioned
for us to eat in healthy,
modern, cholesterol-free
here-we-go-running-
into-the-21st-century
Southern California heat.

But we store bagels in our freezer
for a daily breakfast treat,
as one line of prayer
from a forgotten liturgy.

HEDDA

I lost my unborn child on the railroad tracks
as I ran after my husband
leaving on the troop train,
taken away to fight and die.

That blood was not the last I saw.
In years to come I ate stale potatoes –
never any meat – and lived,
until I, too, was taken
with all the yellow-starred prisoners.

The Nazis told us, "Work will make you free."
"Arbeit macht frei" was inscribed on the gate
to the camp where I sewed, coughed
and spit more blood, and hid from the guards
who kicked me when I fell.
My sister put me in a stack of hay,
fed me scraps so I would live.
When freedom came, we few who lived
sewed back together shattered lives.

Fleeing from one unwanted place to the next
and, finally, to a refuge safe and secure,
I spend days in my few rooms, not able to move.
My cane, walker and wheelchair
support me less each day, as my spine gives in
to a kick from fifty years ago.

The apartment window looking on the street
does not show as much to me as my TV,
which opens up the whole world,
and I can see others, running on other tracks,
in other camps, dying in many ways.
And I still live.

A WEDDING GIFT

The fancy clock, handmade
out of fine wood, inlaid
with George Washington's face
and Mount Vernon home,
is a wedding gift from our oldest aunt,
survivor of Auschwitz,
for our newly married son.

The clock will hang on the wall
above the table where
computer, printer and phone cables
will link his home
with inter-netted millions.

Can I explain to him the links between
Auschwitz, George Washington
and his suburban home?

BONDS
(In Teresa's Voice)

The last of the Israel bonds,
purchased annually by my mother,
rejoicing in her grandchildren,
lie in the dresser drawer
with baby clothes:

Brown woolen sweater knit for me
in Budapest by my grandmother,
who died in Auschwitz
while I survived;

Yellow-striped jumper,
hand sewn for my newborn son
by the Swedish friend who knew me
as an American teacher in Berlin;

White pajamas I made myself
for my baby boy,
now a teacher of young children.

Baby clothes and Israel bonds
lie together, waiting for redemption
into cash for the young teacher
to furnish his new house,
where, perhaps,
baby clothes will lie
in a dresser drawer.

SOUP

When my wife makes soup
to warm her lost childhood years,
she cuts potatoes and carrots,
adds a great big bone,
brings them to a boil,
not in the heavy black-iron pot
her grandmother used
in the Hungarian village,
but in the huge steel-clad one
her mother gave her thirty years ago.

She stirs in caraway seed – the flavor
of Budapest childhood winters –
adds more potatoes
(as many as a week's ration
at Bergen-Belsen),
a handful of pasta,
curved and stout as the women
whose pictures fill the photo albums
rescued from beneath the floor
of the bombed-out home.

She made enough for the two of us tonight,
for leftovers, too,
so we'll never be starved for memories.

Bergen-Belsen was a concentration camp established by Nazi Germany in 1940. In 1944 over
1,500 Hungarian Jews were kept there for ransom. They were released in December 1944 to
internment in Switzerland in exchange for food and medicines.

AM YISRAEL CHAI!
The People Israel Lives!

Out of the depths,
away from smokestacks and ashes,
hiding from sirens,
hidden in cellars,
running in forests,
working in camps,
you survived.

Nishmat Kol Chai...
the souls of all the living
weep for those lost,
while those who lived
bear unknown scars
deep beneath the tattooed arms
and broken bones.

Parents, sisters and brothers,
cousins, all quiet or angry,
old or small,
followed booted horror
and died.
And you survived.

Once-despised dregs
of a continent in flames,
you outlived the horror,
myriads of names
wafted in smoke
or hid in nameless graves.

Now we recall the names
of those who lived,
gave seed, give birth,
survived,
so that today we know
Am Yisrael Chai!

"Nishmat Kol Chai," Hebrew for "Souls of all the living."

MAXIMA

"It's a Mahxima!" Vlad crowed,
stretching the "ah" as broad
as the steppes beyond the Volga.
"See gold coloring they put on this car!"
His rr's bristled like the towering firs
lining the Moskva River,
near his former home.

In the parking lot
outside his apartment,
his pre-teen daughter at his side,
his eyes shone brighter
than the sealed-beam lights
on the Japanese import car
he'd bought to celebrate two years
as an American worker.

In his rolling rugged Russian
he gave directions to Dvora
who went into the apartment,
before he cajoled and dragged us
to his small kitchen table,
where packaged sweets, bread,
soda, vodka, were all laid out
for us to share;
as we had shared his
driving lessons, application forms,
shuttling Dvora to an American school,
and his fears he might never learn
American ways, or she might forget
the speech that had purred
through her early years.

"Yes, it's a Mahxima," we agreed,
thinking more of the great joy
of freely chosen work,
of a home and the means to share
delicious treats with his guests.

AT MANZANAR

the Eastern California Park Service
will build a fence
where, once, barbed wire kept others in,
to keep out grazing cattle – and vandals
who think preserving Manzanar
is un-American.

In the high California desert
ghosted-cabin shadows surround
dusty memories of relocated internees –
Americans born of immigrant Japanese parents,
uprooted, ripped from their farms,
homes and stores of the new Promised Land –

relocated to protect themselves
from the threat of invasion
or the reality of hate.

Ghost shadows surround echoes of quiet chants.
An Ikibana-adorned altar stood here,
dignified center of a stopgap home,
where patient Americans waited
to begin their lives again.

I saw a lone guide appear, standing
by the stone foundation of a sentry house,
to show and tell the history of this place
from the time before the earlier invasion,
when his Paiute Indian ancestors
roamed here,
free.

Manzanar was one of 10 relocation and internment camps established in 1942 by the U.S.
government for Japanese-American citizens in response to the attack on Pearl Harbor. The
Manzanar National Historic Site is located in California, East of Sequoia National Park.

ON THE MOUNTAIN

The body was pulled through the wire fence,
strands lifted by men in uniform.
He was laid on the gurney,
covered by coats and blankets,
and was gently carried
down the snow-topped mountain
to the waiting ambulance.
Pablo cried as he tried to help *la Migra*,
men he once had feared,
who saved his brother Jesus' life.

A springtime walk from a barren home,
with little food to eat, but much hope
to nourish them as they looked for work,
cutting grass or sweeping floors
in the City of Angels, they dared the nights,
the deserts, the surprising cold and heights,
where snow froze their plastic-wrapped feet.

Three days of walking without food,
one of saving warmth in a hospital room,
and again they were removed,
thrust out from this golden land,
where skiers on vacation
and police kindly give clothes
to lost and tattered beggars.

Pablo and Jesus did not meet
on a Damascus road,
but were seeking their own Jerusalem.

"La Migra," colloquial Spanish for U.S. Immigration Service

PORT OF ENTRY

As I look out from my office,
through the twenty-foot-wide window,
onto the road below, I see trucks
and cars and my people
walking, all waiting to go through
the gates to our promised land.

I never dreamed I'd sit by this window,
guarding the road I once walked in hope.
Gatekeepers, in uniforms as I wear,
stand and stare into each car or truck.
They often pull aside a driver
who looks too nervous, too dark,
without good papers, or who traveled
this road too many times this year.

This year…a special one for me.
It's been twenty years
since I came through that gate,
a skinny, nervous *muchacho*
but with a magic letter inviting
me to live with family, citizens
in *El Norte*, the land of dreams.

School, school in two languages,
escuela bilinque, escuela en dos idiomas,
made me an American. When I took
a job, working for *la Migra,*
my family called me traitor
to my people, but soon they knew
I serve the law and serve us well.
Our people will grow free
in our chosen home.

Now I look out my window and see
other dreamers walking, wanting work,
waiting for the time to join me,
buying new clothes, paying taxes,
going to school, speaking American
and voting.

"La Migra," colloquial Spanish for U.S. Immigration Service

CUSTOMS

Each time I drove across the border,
coming home from Canada,
I feared the Customs sign. It meant
I would be stopped, challenged, dared
to prove that America is my home.

Just because my skin is dark,
swarthy as the desert sand
near where my father was born,
I am stopped each time I return
to the land of my birth.

I would remove my license long before
I neared the Customs sign. But I learned
a driver's license is not enough
to convince the uniforms at the gate
that I belong as much as they. I tried
to talk about the football team,
show I am American, but they
think I might be a well-trained spy.

The Customs sign now alerts me
to show my certificate of birth,
just to prove that this land
is my own. But I am sure
as long as I live here, a citizen –
the gift my father gave when I was born –
I'll never learn
the customs.

SOMALIA IN SAN DIEGO

Bronze whiskers mark proud contrast
to his black skin. Graying hair is hid
beneath a figured fez, as ornate
as ancient Sheba's palaces.
He sits at the desk of his twelve-year-old son,
in a school far from the teaching sands
of his homeland.

Eyes peer out from centuries
of remembered scorn, a withering look
to teachers, newsmen,
crossing guards, writers, who visit
this catch-all school, where each morn
children come from concrete egg-crate
tenements to learn new ways,
learn to live in a land not yet torn
by tribal strife.

"What life
lies ahead for our son?"
he asks his wife,
in their quiet private tongue.
"What good can come
from this exodus we've made?"

She lowers her eyes
as she would for any man, and says,
"What good can come?
We have come.
We live!"

PENNSYLVANIA AVENUE, WASHINGTON, D.C.

The fourth-generation shoe-store owner
is proud to be part of the redevelopment
of Pennsylvania Avenue,
modern, sleek, monumental.

He welcomes competition
as he sees marchers,
in protests or inaugural parades,
in this, the richest nation,
always wear shoes.

AT THE OUTLET MALL

in Los Angeles I heard
Hindi from sari-cloaked arms
wrapped in traditions of gold;
Japanese from two chic ladies with cigarettes
finely held by thumb and first finger;
happy Spanish from children
eager to find some special treats.

Overhead, jet planes banked
in instrumented landing patterns,
bringing even more burbling voices
to the malls and streets
of our promised land.

REACH TOMORROW

Her black eyes were wide open
when we met her,
coming through the customs door,
a new bride
coming to join her husband here.

(I remember coming through that door,
scared and alone, fifteen years ago,
with jungle-camp odor still in my clothes.
Now I only smell the nail polish
and remover that I work with.
I love the smell and the polish
of my clean American home.)

My nephew said she's pretty,
but I did not expect to see
such dark beauty look so young and small.
Even though the war was over
when she was born in Saigon,
she never ate the fine food
we eat every day. My teenage son
seems twice as big. But we'll feed her well
before she asks for strange American food.

On the freeway, heading home, I joked
to her and her brand new husband –
a proud American, ten years here
and a citizen, works hard like a millionaire –
I joked that the traffic on our roads
gets worse every day.

       She said, "No!
In Saigon it's worse than here.
There's no room to breathe
between the bikes and busses,
the duk-duks, and old-old French cars,
stinking all the air with fumes and noise.
In America you have big roads, much space,
and room to reach tomorrow."

"Duk-duks," three-wheeled motorbikes found in Asian cities. The name echoes the sound of
the two-cycle engine.

WHAT'S COOKED UP FOR ME?

I know I was selected,
chosen from hundreds of orphans
saved from the streets and markets
of a once war-torn nation,
a country where impurity of race,
a different color or shape
of face or eye, would mark my life
as outcast, not let into schools
or jobs or even marriage,
except with one like me.

I was saved from an unknown fate,
moved across the sea, to this land
where many still believe that color,
race or shape of face should not predict
the future of a child. In school
they called me "Chink" and other names,
not knowing or caring which Asian land
was my place of birth. I didn't know
or care to learn Asian words. I dreamed
to be like my new parents and their friends.
I didn't want to eat the rice
and Asian food folks offered me –
kim chee, pho or sashimi.
I chose fried chicken, burgers, pizza –
American food, so I could be
like my cousins and the guys
I wanted for friends at school.

But I guess someday I'll try to learn a bit
about where I was born. I can't enjoy
my mom's bratwurst or my dad's
French sauces and call those my heritage.
I need to know what's cooked up for me.
Where do I belong?

CAFE AU LAIT

"When we all look like café au lait,"
my uncle said, "hate will disappear.
No more black or white, or golden tan,
what some call yellow but does not match
the sun in radiance."

I guess when cream mixed
with coffee's wakening black
describes us all, no one will fear
or even know a different kind.

We'll need to look inside
to find those tantalizing traits
that make you different, that make me me.
But when we are all as café au lait,
what will happen if I meet one
who is like orange pekoe tea?

GOLDEN WHEAT

Golden wheat replaces
the golden streets
of hope, as smuggled human cargo
spill out of a sliding van
on a rainy Nebraska highway.

Transcontinental coyotes
heading for minimum wage Chicago
from bordertown Arizona
lose their investment
to the surprised Omaha office
of *la Migra*.

Smuggled cargo and their smugglers,
returned to Mexico,
will try again,
for they have smelled
the golden wheat.

"Coyotes" is the idiom used to describe smugglers who traffic in illegal human cargo, as they
generally travel at night.
"La Migra," colloquial Spanish for U.S. Immigration Service

FREED, DELIVERED, REDEEMED

"Where did I come from?" the boy asked.
His father replied, "The question should be
we, not *I.* We came from other places.
We were freed from Kishinev and Chiapas,
delivered from Tien-an-mien, Saigon,
from Zanzibar and Timbuktu, and all
slave places infected with hate
of one people for another.

"We were redeemed from Austerlitz and Guernica,
from Auschwitz and Teheran,
from Armenia, Gaza and Bosnia,
from auto-da-fé and Crusades.

"We have escaped the hate
and have been brought
to this magic land, where
we must always know
where we came from."

See Exodus 6:5-8.

A SECOND TONGUE

Do I have a second tongue,
another language than the one
I learned at mother's side?

When I hear a stranger's speech
or read a poem from faraway land,
I reach to grasp the thought
cast in words I do not know or understand
and listen for the heartbeat,
the sigh, the gasp of breath,
that unexpressed "I"
which moved another's pen to write
or mouth to speak.

Then I hear and know those thoughts
that flow across time and space
teach me to fine-tune an inner ear,
allow me to understand
there is no foreign tongue,
no strange land,
no alien race.

THANK YOU NOTES

Darwin was right!
The strongest do survive!
They leave their low estate
where there's no free air to breathe,
no honest work to feed themselves.

The strong and fit will find a way,
nightwalking across a hidden stream,
crowding on a smuggler's boat,
living hope in a jungle camp,
reborn to freedom from a secret womb
of a carved-out car,
waiting in endless visa lines
to escape a gulag nation.
Their power drives them forward
as pistons drive the engine arms
that move the world.

Some marry the American dream;
others are adopted as dreamt-for children.

This golden land receives the gifts
of their strength, their genes, their sacred blood.

We whose lives are blessed
by fair elections,
open land to travel free,
by clean water, schools and work,
should send thank you notes
to Brezhnev, Castro, Jiang, Saddam –
dictators, autocrats, despots,
thieves and commissars –
who drove their best and brightest
to our shores.

ABOUT THE AUTHOR

Merle Fischlowitz was born and grew up in St. Louis, Mo. His parents were also born in St. Louis in the first decade of the 20th Century. Merle's four grandparents had all come to St. Louis as young, single persons in the 1880s from Poland and Lithuania. He first met immigrant refugees from Europe, including some cousins, both before and after World War II. His father and his uncle sponsored their Viennese refugee relatives in 1938, just as their father and uncles had sponsored refugee cousins after the flu epidemic in Europe in 1919.

When Merle attended Grinnell College in Iowa, he enjoyed knowing and learning from the many international students there. At Grinnell, he majored in History and Psychology, planning to become a history teacher.

During his career as educator and psychologist in Missouri, Maryland and Hawaii, Merle enjoyed many friendships with new Americans and descendants of immigrant families.

In 1975 Merle and his former wife adopted a three-year-old boy from Vietnam. That son is Benjamin, an artist whose work is on the cover of this book. Merle's present wife, Teresa, is also an immigrant and is one of the youngest survivors from Bergen-Belsen concentration camp in Germany. Teresa's family was part of a group of 1,500 Hungarian Jews who managed to be ransomed out of Germany in December 1944.

Merle has written poetry since high school and enjoys using words to express his deep commitment to the United States and its people. He and Teresa now live in San Diego. They share six grown children and four grandchildren.